EASY-TO-DO CRAFTS • EASY-TO-FIND THINGS

175 Easy-to-Do EASTER CRAFTS

Edited by Sharon Dunn Umnik

P9-DMJ-753

BOYDS MILLS PRESS

Inside this book . . .

you'll find a fabulous assortment of crafts made from recyclable items and inexpensive things found in or around your house. Have pencils, crayons, scissors, tape, and other supplies for craft making close by. – *the Editor*

Published by Bell Books
Boyds Mills Press, Inc.
A Highlights Company
815 Church Street
Honesdale, Pennsylvania 18431
Printed in the United States of America

Publisher Cataloging-in-Publication Data
Main entry under title :
   175 easy-to-do Easter crafts : easy-to-do crafts, easy-to-find things /
edited by Sharon Dunn Umnik.—1st ed.
[64]p. : col. photo. ; cm.
Includes index.
Summary : Includes step-by-step directions to make and decorate Easter baskets, eggs, rabbits, place cards, greeting cards, and more.
ISBN 1-56397-316-2
1. Handicraft—Juvenile literature. 2. Easter decorations—Juvenile literature. [1. Handicraft. 2. Easter decorations.] I. Umnik, Sharon Dunn.
II. Title.
J 745.594 dc20   1994   CIP
Library of Congress Catalog Card Number 93-70871

First edition, 1994
Book designed by Charlie Cary
The text of this book is set in 11-point New Century Schoolbook.
Distributed by St. Martin's Press

10 9 8 7 6 5 4 3 2 1

Craft Contributors: Jennifer and Caroline Arnold, Patricia Barley, Katherine Corliss Bartow, Linda Bloomgren, Barr Clay Bullock, Mary Caldwell, Catherine Carmody, Catherine Chase, Mindy Cheraz, Ann Clark, Mary Colarico, Carol Conner, Kathleen Conrad, Evelyn Cook, Paige Eckard, Laurie Edwards, Donna L. Eichler, Gladys Emerson, Virginia Follis, Dee Francis, Sarah T. Frey, Sandra Godfrey, Mavis Grant, Mildred Grenier, Norah Grubmeyer, Edna Harrington, Joann M. Hart, Ann Hatch, Kathryn Heisenfelt, Texie Hering, Loretta Holz, Carmen Horn, Olive Howie, Tama Kain, Virginia Killough, Garnett Kooker, Judith L. LaDez, Twilla Lamm, Sarah V. Lasher, Ruth E. Libbey, Lee Lindeman, Alvera M. Lundin, M. Mable Lunz, Agnes Maddy, Patricia A. McMillan, Ursula Michael, Patty S. Milton, June Rose Mobly, Judith Morgan, Ellen E. Morrison, Sister Mary Norma, Anita Page, Dorothe A. Palms, S. Peoples, Beatrice Bachrach Perri, James W. Perrin Jr., Luella Pierce, Ellen Plausky, Jane K. Priewe, Karla P. Ray, Terry A. Ricioli, Kathy Ross, Barbara Smith, Mary Collette Spees, June Swanson, Sister Mary Sylvia, V.S.C., Mildred G. Turner, Sharon Dunn Umnik, Jan J. Van Pelt, Bernice Walz, Jean White, Pamela Young Wolff, Agnes Choate Wonson, Jinx Woolson, and Connie Wright.

Gigantic EASTER EGGS

PEEK-A-BOO EGG
(plastic-foam trays, plastic grass,
permanent markers, felt, fabric trim)

Follow the steps below, then
cut a hole in one side of the
egg. Draw and cut out two
rabbits and an Easter basket
with pointed bottoms from
plastic-foam trays. Decorate
them with felt and permanent
markers. Place some plastic
grass inside the egg with the
rabbits and their basket. Glue
some fabric trim around the
hole and hang up the egg.

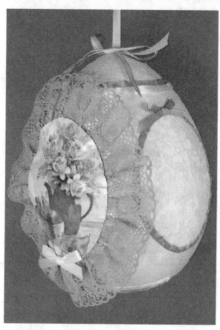

VICTORIAN EGG
(old greeting card, lace, ribbon)

Follow the steps below, then
cut a scene from an old
greeting card in the shape of
an oval. Glue it to one side of
the egg. Cut three oval shapes
from lace, and glue them to
the other sides of the egg.
Decorate the egg with more
ribbon.

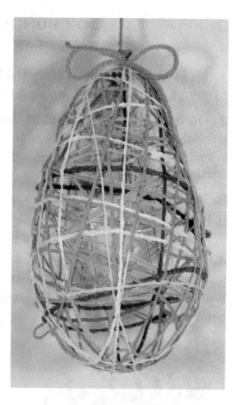

YARN EGG
(different-colored yarn)

Follow the steps below, except
instead of using white tissue
paper, dip different-colored
lengths of yarn into the
mixture. Wrap the yarn
around an inflated balloon
and let dry. Pop the balloon
and pull it out from between
the yarn. Attach a yarn
hanger.

BASIC STEPS FOR MAKING A GIANT EASTER EGG
(egg-shaped balloons, a large plastic food container, glue, water, white tissue paper, string)

1. Make a mixture of equal amounts of white glue
and water in a large plastic food container. Blow
up an egg-shaped, light-colored balloon and knot
the end. Tie a piece of string around the knot.

2. Tear strips of white tissue paper, and dip them
into the mixture. Cover the balloon with the
strips.

3. Hang the balloon to dry. Add more layers,
letting each one dry before adding another.

4. Pop the balloon and pull it out of the egg shape
by pulling gently on the string. Cover the hole
where the balloon knot was with paper and glue
if needed. Place a piece of yarn or ribbon at the
same spot for a hanger. Add layers of tissue
paper, letting each dry as before, to cover the hole
and to hold the ribbon in place.

**NOTE: Always cover your work surface, and
be sure to clean up your mess.**

BOX BUNNY SURPRISE
(quart-size milk carton, construction paper, tissue paper)

1. Measure 2 1/2 inches from the bottom of a quart-size milk carton, and draw a line around the carton.

2. On one side, draw a rabbit's head above the line. Cut around the rabbit's head and then on the line around the three other sides. Cut and glue a strip of construction paper around the carton.

3. Lay the rabbit side down on a piece of paper, and trace around it twice. Cut out the rabbit shapes. Glue one to the outside, covering the carton, and glue the other one to the inside.

4. Cut out eyes, a mouth, a nose, whiskers, and ears from paper, and glue them on the bunny. Line the "bunny box" with tissue paper, and fill with nuts, cookies, or candy for a holiday surprise.

EASTER EGG CARD
(poster board, yarn)

1. Fold a piece of poster board in half to make a card.

2. Draw and cut out an egg shape from another piece of poster board. Spread several lines of white glue on the egg shape, dividing it into sections. Press black yarn into the glue.

3. Fill the sections with glue, and press pieces of yarn into the glue, starting at the outline of each section and moving toward the middle.

4. Glue the yarn egg to the front of the card. Write a holiday message.

EASTER MOBILE
(yarn, two wooden sticks, poster board)

1. Place two wooden sticks together to form an X. Wrap yarn around the center, adding glue. Add a yarn loop for hanging.

2. Cut four eggs, four chicks, and a rabbit from white poster board. Decorate them with markers or crayons. Punch a hole in the top of each shape.

3. Using short pieces of yarn, tie the eggs to the ends of the sticks. Using longer pieces of yarn, tie the chicks halfway between the ends and the center. Using an even longer piece of yarn, tie the rabbit to the center of the X.

4. Slide the shapes along the sticks until the mobile hangs evenly.

GIFT BAG
(brown paper bag, yarn, old greeting card)

1. Cut a picture from an old greeting card, and glue it onto a brown paper bag. Write a message. Place a gift inside.

2. Fold about 1 inch of the bag's top inside. Close the bag and punch four holes across the top. String a piece of yarn through the holes and tie a bow.

SPOON-FLOWER PLACE CARD
(plastic spoon, 1-inch plastic-foam ball, poster board, toothpicks)

1. Paint the bowl part of a plastic spoon to look like a flower and let it dry. Paint the handle to look like the stem of the flower.

2. Press a 1-inch plastic-foam ball against a hard surface to flatten one side. Glue it to a piece of poster board. Push the stem of the flower into the top of the ball.

3. Cut leaves from poster board, and glue each leaf onto a toothpick, leaving the pointed end of the toothpick showing on the bottom. Push the leaves into the ball next to the stem.

4. Write a name on a piece of poster board. Glue it to a small piece of toothpick, and push it into the ball in front of the flower.

A GIFT THAT GROWS
(yarn, plastic food container)

1. Spread an inch of glue around the outside bottom of a plastic food container.

2. Working from the bottom, press the end of a piece of yarn into the glue, and start winding it around the container. Use different colors of yarn. Glue a decoration on the front and let it dry.

3. Place small stones in the bottom of the container for drainage. Add some dirt and clippings from a growing plant, or place a potted plant in the container.

FELT EASTER EGGS
(felt, lace, ribbon, cotton balls)

1. For each egg, cut two ovals from felt. Glue lace or ribbon on the ovals for decoration.

2. Turn the ovals to the undecorated side. Spread glue on the edges of the ovals, and place a few cotton balls in the center of one oval.

3. Place the second oval on top of the first, pressing the ovals together at the edges.

COTTON-BALL RABBIT
(cardboard, felt, buttons, black yarn, string, cotton balls)

1. Draw and cut out a rabbit shape from cardboard. Cover the ears with pieces of pink felt. Outline them with glue and cotton balls.

2. Spread glue over the rest of the rabbit, and completely cover it with cotton balls.

3. From felt, cut out and glue on eyes, a nose, and a bow tie. Glue buttons onto the body. Glue on black yarn for the mouth.

4. Attach a piece of short string to the top of the rabbit for a hanger.

GIFT WRAP EASTER CARD
(construction paper, gift wrap)

1. On a piece of folded construction paper, draw and cut out an egg shape, with the left side on the fold.

2. Cut out flower shapes from bits of gift wrap paper, and glue them to the front of the egg. Cut a vase and leaves from construction paper, and glue them in place. Use a marker to draw stems.

3. Write an Easter message inside the card.

EASTER WREATH
(cardboard, yarn, plastic-foam trays, glitter)

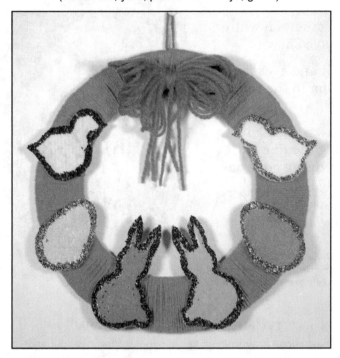

1. Cut a doughnut shape from cardboard to make a wreath. Wrap yarn completely around it.

2. Draw and cut out chicks, rabbits, and eggs from plastic-foam trays. Spread glue around the edges of each shape, sprinkle them with glitter, and let dry. Glue the shapes to the wreath.

3. Add a yarn bow for decoration. Attach a loop of yarn to the back of the wreath for a hanger.

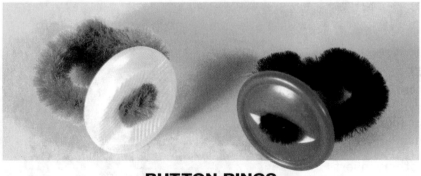

BUTTON RINGS
(pipe cleaners, buttons with two large holes)

1. Using a button with two large holes, push a pipe cleaner through one hole and back down through the other.

2. Twist the ends of the pipe cleaner together, adjusting the ring to the size of your finger.

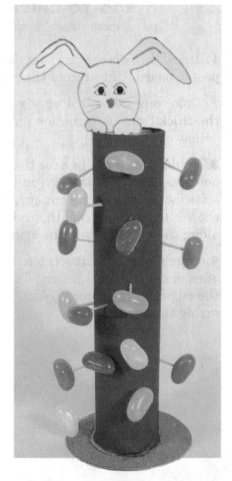

JELLY-BEAN POLE
(paper towel tube, cardboard, poster paint, construction paper, toothpicks, jelly beans)

1. Cut a paper towel tube to measure 7 inches in length. To make a base, cut a small cardboard circle and glue it to one end of the tube. Cover with poster paint and let dry.

2. Use the tip of a ball-point pen to poke holes around the tube. Put a jelly bean on one end of a toothpick, and stick the other end of the toothpick into a hole.

3. Draw and cut out a small bunny and glue it to the inside of the tube, so the bunny appears to be peeking over the top.

EGG-TO-CHICK EASTER CARD
(poster board, construction paper, gift wrap)

1. Draw three large egg shapes, touching each other, on white poster board. Cut around them to make the shape shown.

2. Color one side of the eggs yellow. Make a bill and eyes for the chick from construction paper, and glue them to the center yellow egg.

3. Fold the outer eggs over the center one. Draw a zigzag line down the center of the egg on top, and cut along the line with scissors. Fold over the cut egg, trace along the zigzag edge on the white egg underneath, and then cut along the edge. Unfold the eggs.

4. Glue a piece of gift wrap to the outside of each egg half and let dry. Trim around the edges with scissors. Write a message inside the card.

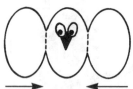

Fold over on dotted line

STAINED-GLASS WINDOW
(plastic-foam tray, colored tissue paper, glitter, newspaper)

1. Draw an outline of a stained-glass window design on a plastic-foam tray. Press out the sections of the window with a dull table knife.

2. Cut pieces of colored tissue paper slightly larger than the cutout sections of the window. Tape these pieces to the back of the tray, covering the cutout section.

3. On a work area covered with newspaper, spread glue on the outline of the window, and sprinkle with glitter. Add a yarn loop to hang in a window.

MINI EASTER BASKET
(plastic food container, two pipe cleaners, fabric, ribbon, plastic grass)

1. Punch a hole on both sides of a plastic food container near the top with a paper punch.

2. Wrap two pipe cleaners around each other, insert each end into a hole, and twist the ends together for the handle.

3. Glue fabric and ribbon to the outside of the container.

4. Decorate the handle with ribbon and a bow. Fill the basket with plastic grass and treats.

BABY BUNNY

(washcloth, rubber band, ribbon, moveable plastic eyes,
string, yarn, cotton ball)

1. Place a washcloth on the table in front of you. Tightly roll one corner to the center. Hold the rolled section in place while you turn the washcloth around and roll the opposite corner toward the center. (See Diagram 1.)

2. With the rolled side down, fold the washcloth in half. (See Diagram 2.) Then fold back about 2 inches from one end. Place a rubber band around this section to form the bunny's head. (See Diagram 3.) Tie a ribbon over the rubber band.

3. Add moveable plastic eyes, a yarn nose, and string whiskers to the head. Glue on a cotton ball for a tail.

Diagram 1   Diagram 2   Diagram 3

EGG-CARTON NUT CUP

(cardboard egg carton, construction paper)

1. Cut one cup section from a cardboard egg carton. Scallop the edge with a pair of scissors.

2. For a base, draw and cut out the green leafy part of a flower from construction paper. Then cut a flower with long petals. Glue the leaf section and the flower together.

3. Glue the scalloped cup section to the middle of the base. Put peanuts in the cup.

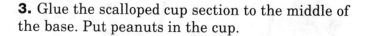

EASTER RABBIT HAT

(poster board, paper doily, construction paper)

1. Cut a rabbit head from poster board. Add pink ears from construction paper.

2. Glue a small paper doily over the rabbit's head. Add paper eyes, nose, mouth, and whiskers to the face.

3. Cut a long strip of poster board, and glue the rabbit to the center of the strip. Staple the ends of the strip together so that it fits on your head.

BUNNY PARTY CUP

(plastic-foam cup, construction paper, yarn)

1. Draw bunny ears on the middle of a plastic-foam cup. Cut the cup in half, cutting around the bunny ears.

2. Paper-punch two black eyes from construction paper, and glue them to the cup below the ears.

3. Cut pieces of yarn, and glue them on as whiskers. Add other features with a marker, and glue on a cotton-ball tail.

STAND-UP EASTER CARD

(poster board)

1. Fold a long piece of poster board in half. Open the card, and draw an egg on the bottom half just below the fold. On the top half, just above the fold, draw a chick coming out of the egg.

2. Write a message on the egg, and color the drawing with crayons or markers. Cut around the outline of the chick with scissors just to the fold of the paper. Fold back the card so it will stand up.

CHICK IN A NEST

(cardboard egg carton, yarn, an eggshell half, construction paper, paint)

1. Cut a cup section from a cardboard egg carton. Spread glue around the outside of the cup. Press the end of a piece of yarn into the glue, and wind the yarn around the cup.

2. Glue pieces of yellow yarn inside the nest for straw. Paint half of an eggshell.

3. Add features cut from paper, and glue the chick inside the nest.

EASTER PLACE MAT
(construction paper)

1. Place a sheet of construction paper 12 inches by 18 inches lengthwise in front of you. Cut vertical slits 8 inches long and 2 1/2 inches apart.

2. Using paper of another color, cut three strips 2 1/2 inches by 18 inches. Weave them in and out of the slits on the large sheet of paper to form a checkerboard pattern. Glue down the ends of the strips.

3. Decorate some of the squares with decorated paper eggs.

FAN FLOWERS
(fabric, pipe cleaners)

1. Cut a piece of fabric 2 1/2 inches wide and 8 inches long. Starting at the narrow end, fold over 1/3 of an inch and continue to fold into accordion pleats until the entire piece is pleated.

2. Bend one end of a long pipe cleaner around the center of the folded fabric, and twist it to make the flower and stem. Pull the folded flower open into a circle.

3. For the leaves, loop and twist short pieces of pipe cleaner onto the stem. Make several flowers, and place them in a vase.

HOLIDAY BELT
(plastic lids, permanent marker, pipe cleaners, yarn)

1. Cut egg and tulip shapes from plastic lids, such as those used on coffee, margarine, peanut, or cereal containers. Color the edges of the eggs and tulips with a permanent marker.

2. Punch a hole at the edge of each shape, and join them with pieces of pipe cleaners or yarn. Continue to make as many shapes as you need to go around your waist.

3. At each end of the belt, tie on a longer piece of yarn to fasten the belt around your waist.

STAND-UP DECORATION
(construction paper)

1. Fold a 6-inch-by-8-inch piece of construction paper in half the long way, then across. Measure 1/2 inch up from the longer unfolded side and draw a line for the base.

2. At the folded side, draw half an egg on the base as shown. Beside the egg, draw a chick with the head touching the top fold and the bottom touching the base. Cut through all four layers and unfold.

3. Add details to the chicks with markers. Draw a decorative border, and write a name on the egg. Stand the decoration up by opening the bottom slightly.

EGG HEADBAND
(poster board, poster paint)

1. Cut a strip of poster board about 3 inches wide and long enough to go around your head, overlapping the ends a little. Tape or glue the ends together.

2. Cut out egg-shaped pieces from poster board. Decorate them with poster paint. When the eggs are dry, glue them evenly around the band.

BUNNY EASTER BASKET
(two plastic-foam egg cartons of the same color, one cardboard egg carton, cotton balls, construction paper, fabric)

1. Cut off the tops of both plastic-foam cartons and cut one of the bottoms in half the long way, making a row of six cups. Glue this row, upside down, over half of the other foam carton, leaving the other half open for the basket.

2. Decorate the row of egg shapes with cotton noses and paper whiskers, eyes, and heart shapes for feet. Make ears from paper, and glue one pair to the back of each bunny head.

3. On every other bunny, glue on a bow of fabric to the top of the head.

4. Cut little hats from the cardboard carton's peaked dividers. Paint them black, and glue each to a circle of black paper. Glue the hats to the remaining bunny heads.

FLOWER PIN
(seeds from fruit or sunflowers, lightweight cardboard,
popcorn kernels, felt, safety pin)

1. Wash and dry seeds from apples, melons, lemons, or sunflowers.

2. Cut a circle from lightweight cardboard.

3. Glue a row of seeds, with their points toward the center, around the outer edge of the circle. Glue on another row of seeds, overlapping the first row. Continue with three or four rows.

4. Glue popcorn kernels in the center.

5. Glue on green felt leaves and a safety pin to the back of the cardboard.

COFFEE-FILTER FLOWERS
(coffee filters, food coloring, pipe cleaners)

1. For each flower, fold a coffee filter into quarters. Dampen the filter with water. Add drops of food coloring onto the filter in any pattern.

2. Press the filter between pieces of waxed paper to spread the color. Open the filter, and let it dry on paper towels.

3. Fold the filter in quarters again, forming a point at the bottom. Twist a pipe cleaner around the point for a stem.

WOOLLY LAMB
(poster board, yarn, moveable plastic eyes)

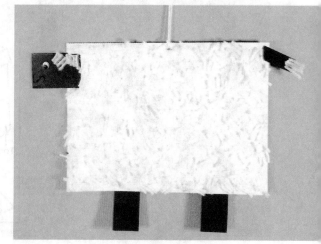

1. For the body of the lamb, cut a rectangle from white poster board. Cut three strips of black poster board and fold in half for the legs and the head of the lamb.

2. Cut one more black strip, smaller in size, and fold it in half for the tail of the lamb. Glue the legs, tail, and head to the white poster board. Add moveable plastic eyes and a piece of yarn for the mouth.

3. Spread glue on the white poster board and sprinkle on cut pieces of white yarn, covering the entire lamb. Glue a loop of yarn to the back for a hanger.

RUB-A-PICTURE
(crayon, cardboard, construction paper)

1. Cut shapes such as rabbits, eggs, chicks, or flowers from cardboard. Glue them on a sheet of construction paper.

2. Place a sheet of construction paper over the cardboard picture. Rub over the paper with the side of a crayon. Watch the picture appear.

3. The rabbit pictured here shows how the different parts are cut and glued. The overlapping parts are brought out in detail in the rubbed picture.

EASTER BASKET
(cereal box, construction paper, plastic grass)

1. Cut a large corner section from the bottom of a cereal box to make the top of the basket. Cut a smaller corner section from the bottom to make the bottom of the basket. Cover both pieces with glue and construction paper.

2. Cut the point off the bottom corner section of the basket as shown.

3. Turn the large corner section so the opening is up, and glue the bottom into the opening of the bottom section.

4. Decorate the basket with paper. Cut strips of construction paper, and glue them to the basket to make a handle.

BUNNY PUPPET
(construction paper, two spring-type clothespins, old sock)

1. From paper, cut out bunny ears long enough to cover spring-type clothespins. Glue the ears to the clothespins.

2. Lay an old sock on a table. Cut out eyes, nose, and whiskers from paper. Glue them to the bottom of the sock.

3. Place your hand inside the sock, and clip the bunny ears to the heel of the sock.

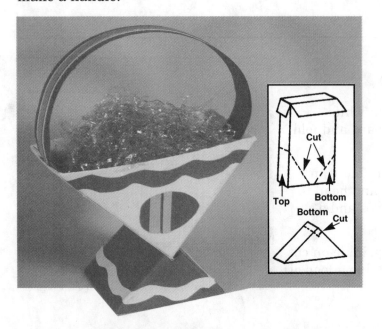

EASTER BRACELET
(plastic-foam cup, yarn, felt)

1. Draw a line about 1 inch from the top edge of a plastic-foam cup. Cut around the cup on the line, making the bracelet form.

2. Wrap yarn around the bracelet. Glue the ends to the inside. Glue on flowers cut from felt.

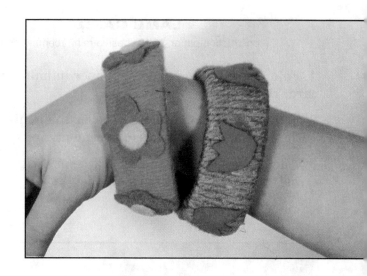

HYACINTH DECORATION
(pinecone, plastic top, colored aluminum foil, tissue paper, ribbon)

1. Glue a pinecone upright in a plastic top covered with colored aluminum foil.

2. Cut tissue paper into 1 1/2-inch squares. Put the point of a pencil in the center of the tissue. Gently twist the paper around the pencil point. Dip the tip into glue, and stick it between the petals of the pinecone.

3. Add a ribbon bow and leaves cut from green paper.

COTTON-BALL SHEEP FAMILY
(cardboard, cotton balls, felt, ribbon)

1. For each sheep, cut two matching sheep shapes from cardboard. Glue the shapes together except for the feet.

2. Glue cotton balls on both sides of the sheep. From felt, cut ears, eyes, cheeks, a nose, a mouth, and feet. Glue them on the sheep. Add a ribbon to each sheep.

3. Bend the feet out a little, until the sheep can stand.

LAMB CARD

(construction paper, self-adhesive reinforcement rings)

1. Fold a piece of construction paper in half to make a card. Draw a lamb on the front.

2. To make its wool look curly, cover the lamb's body with many self-adhesive reinforcement rings.

3. Add grass, flowers, and other scenery with crayons or markers. Write a message inside.

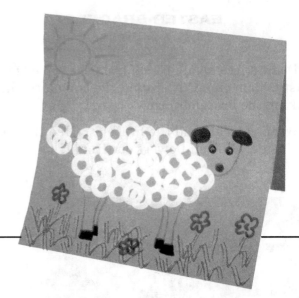

AN EASTER EGG TO HATCH

(poster board, brass fastener)

1. Draw and cut out an egg shape on a piece of poster board. Draw designs on the egg with markers. Cut the egg in half along a jagged line.

2. Draw and cut out a chick from poster board. Glue the chick to the back of the bottom half of the eggshell so that it seems to be sitting in the shell.

3. Attach the top half of the egg to the bottom half with a brass fastener. The egg can then be opened and closed.

RABBIT BOX-PUPPET

(individual-sized cereal box, construction paper, pipe cleaner)

1. Tape the openings of an individual-sized cereal box closed, and cover the box with construction paper.

2. Cut through the box at the center, leaving the back uncut. Cut and glue paper features for the rabbit's face, using the cut at the center as its mouth.

3. Cut pieces from a pipe cleaner and glue them on for whiskers. Cut ears from paper and glue them to the rabbit's head.

4. Cut two small holes through the back, one at the top for your index finger and one at the bottom for your thumb to fit into. Work the puppet with your fingers inside the holes.

FORK-FLOWER CORSAGE

(thick yarn, four-pronged fork, cardboard, construction paper, safety pin)

1. For each flower, weave a piece of thick yarn, about 2 feet long, through a four-pronged fork to make the flowers. Start at the base of the prongs, and weave in a figure 8 pattern by placing the yarn in front of the first two prongs. Then slip the yarn between the second and third prongs; wrap it behind the third and fourth prongs, then in front of them, back between the second and third prongs, behind the first and second prongs, in front of them, and so on. Continue until the fork is full of yarn.

2. Insert an 8-inch piece of green yarn below the wrapped yarn between the second and third prongs. Wrap the green yarn one time around all the yarn on the fork, and tie it loosely.

3. Slip all the yarn off the fork, and tighten the knot. Trim the excess yarn with scissors. Make flowers in a variety of colors, and glue them to a small piece of cardboard.

4. Glue leaves made from construction paper around the flowers. Glue a safety pin to the back of the corsage.

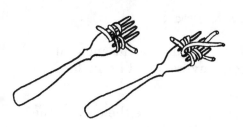

PATCHWORK FLOWERPOT

(fabric, flowerpot)

1. Cut an assortment of colorful scraps of fabric into 1-inch pieces.

2. Spread glue on a small area of the flowerpot and press the pieces of fabric into the glue. Continue until the entire flowerpot is covered.

3. When the fabric is dry, place a flower into the patchwork flowerpot.

CHICK FINGER-PUPPET

(bathroom tissue tube, poster paint, construction paper)

1. Cut points at one end of a bathroom tissue tube. Paint the outside of the tube with poster paint and let dry.

2. Cut a diamond-shaped bill, eyes, and feathers from construction paper. Glue them to the tube.

3. Place a couple of fingers in the bottom of the tube to work the chick puppet.

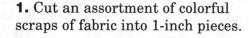

MY LOVE GROWS
(construction paper, package of flower seeds)

1. For the card, fold a piece of construction paper in half. Fold up a strip about 2 inches from the bottom to make a pocket inside.

2. Decorate the front of the card with markers.

3. Place a package of flower seeds in the pocket inside the card and write a message.

BUNNY NECKLACE
(thread spool, cotton balls, felt, yarn, plastic lid)

1. Make a small loop of yarn. Glue the cut ends into the hole of a thread spool, leaving about an inch of the loop sticking up.

2. Cut two ears from a plastic lid. Glue the ears to the spool. Cover the spool with cotton balls.

3. Cut features from felt and attach them with glue.

4. Thread yarn through the loop for the necklace.

HANGING CHICK-BASKET
(two paper plates, two cupcake liners, cardboard, tissue paper, construction paper, plastic grass, ribbon)

1. For the body, staple two paper plates together about two-thirds of the way around with the bottoms of the two plates facing out. Fold down the unstapled part of each plate to form wings and staple in place.

2. For the head, flatten two cupcake liners and glue them together with a circle of cardboard in the middle to stiffen them. Staple it to one end of the body.

3. Cut tissue paper into 1-inch squares. Wrap each square around your finger. Dip the tip in glue and stick it onto the chick's body.

4. Cut a beak and eyes from construction paper, and glue them to the head. Stuff the basket with plastic grass. Punch a hole on each side, and tie a ribbon for a hanger.

EASTER TOP HAT
(poster board, ribbon)

1. To make the top of the hat, cut out a piece of poster board 8 inches long and wide enough to fit around your head. Staple and tape the two ends together. Place the top on another piece of poster board, and draw around the circle.

2. Measure about 2 inches out from the circle, and draw another circle. Cut out on both lines as shown, making the brim. Use 1-inch pieces of tape to fasten the brim to the top.

3. At the other end of the top hat, brush glue around the poster board edge. Place it on another piece of poster board. Add more glue to the inside of the hat and let dry. Trim off the extra board with scissors.

4. Glue a ribbon around the brim of the hat.

EGG-CARTON TULIPS
(cardboard egg carton, poster paint, pipe cleaners, large frozen juice container, construction paper, yarn)

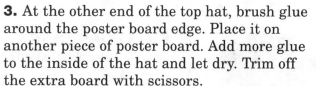

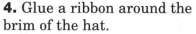

1. To make the flowers, cut out the cup sections from a cardboard egg carton. Trim the corners, making the shape of a tulip petal. Cover the cups with poster paint and let dry.

2. Poke a hole in the bottom of each cup. Push a pipe cleaner through the hole for a stem. Tie a knot about 1 inch away from the other end for the stamen. Add glue and let dry.

3. Cover a large frozen juice container with construction paper. Wrap yarn around the container and tie a bow. Cut long tulip leaves from paper, and place them in the container along with the tulips.

RABBIT STITCHERY
(plastic-foam tray, paper, pen, large-eyed needle, yarn)

1. Wash and dry a plastic-foam tray. On a piece of paper smaller than the tray, draw a rabbit.

2. Tape the picture on the inside of the tray. Poke holes along the lines of the rabbit with a pen. Remove the paper.

French Knot

3. With a needle and yarn, weave in and out of the holes using straight stitches or French knots as shown. Attach a piece of yarn for a hanger.

Straight Stitch

EASTER EGG MOBILE

(plastic-foam egg carton, colored tissue paper, string, wide plastic food container, yarn)

1. Cut cups from a plastic-foam egg carton. For each egg, glue two cups together.

2. Cut designs from colored tissue paper, and glue them to the eggs.

3. Attach a string to each egg for a hanger. Tie all the eggs to a ring cut from a plastic container.

4. Punch four evenly spaced holes in the ring, and tie a length of yarn into each hole. Tie the pieces of yarn together at the top to hang the mobile.

ENVELOPE CHICK

(small white envelope, paper)

1. Open the flap of a small white envelope. With the back of the envelope facing you, draw the eyes and beak of a chick on the flap.

2. Draw wings along the two inner edges of the side flaps.

3. Color your chick yellow and glue it to a piece of paper. Draw legs on the paper.

4. Write your greeting on a piece of paper, and tuck it in the envelope.

PAPER-PLATE RABBIT

(two paper plates, construction paper, cotton, pipe cleaners, yarn)

1. Use one paper plate for the rabbit's head. Cut another paper plate as shown to make the ears and a bow tie. Staple them to the head.

2. Cut a nose, ear centers, and eyes from construction paper. Glue them in place. Glue cotton around the features.

3. Add whiskers made from pipe cleaners. Color the bow tie.

4. Punch a hole at the top of the head, and tie a piece of yarn through the hole for a hanger.

Bow Tie   Ears

CURLY LITTLE LAMB

(bathroom tissue tube,
black and white paper)

1. Cut a bathroom tissue tube to measure about 2 1/2 inches long. Roll a 4-inch-wide piece of black paper and insert it into one end of the tube with about 1 1/2 inches sticking out.

2. Crease the paper and cut out the shape of a head. Glue the sides together. Cut a slit and glue on paper ears. Add eyes.

3. Roll four 1/2-inch-wide pieces of black paper very tightly for the legs. Poke four holes in the tube and insert the legs, adding glue.

4. Cut a piece of white paper the same length as the lamb's body. Make it long enough to go over the body and hang down. Cut two more sheets of paper, each one a little shorter than the last. Cut slits at the ends as shown.

5. Curl the slits by rolling them over a pencil. Glue the curled sheets of paper so the curls are turned under. Glue on the longest sheet first and the shortest sheet last.

Slits

Slit   Ears

HOLIDAY EGG BASKET

(eight ice-cream sticks,
glitter, paint, plastic-foam trays,
permanent markers, plastic grass,
plastic berry basket)

1. Paint eight ice-cream sticks with paint.

2. Cut out eight eggs from plastic-foam trays. Decorate them with glue and glitter. Glue the eggs to the ends of the sticks.

3. Weave the sticks through the sides of a plastic berry basket. Add plastic grass.

FABRIC EASTER BAG

(fabric, tape, pins, embroidery floss,
embroidery needle, felt, shoelace)

1. Cut a piece of fabric about 22 inches long and 14 inches wide. Fold a 3/4-inch hem at each short end. Use pieces of tape or pins to hold in place. Sew together with embroidery floss using straight stitches as shown on page 19.

2. Cut flowers, stems, and leaves from felt. Sew them to the top half of the fabric. Leave a 2-inch border around the edges. Turn the flower side over. Fold a 3/4-inch hem on each long side and hold with tape or pins.

3. With the right side out, fold the fabric in half. Stitch the sides together. Turn the bag inside out, and remove the tape or pins.

4. To make the handle, cut two pieces from a long shoelace. Sew one piece to each side of the bag.

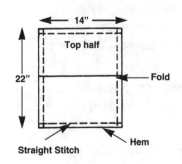

14"

Top half

22"   Fold

Straight Stitch   Hem

POT OF LILIES
(plastic-foam cup, aluminum foil, ribbon, construction paper, clay, pipe cleaners, tissue paper)

1. For each lily, draw and cut a circle from construction paper. Cut a slit to the center of each circle. Glue the ends together, making a cone shape. Cut six small points around the edge of each lily. Curl the points back by rolling them around a pencil.

2. Cut a tiny hole in the pointed end of each lily. Curl one end of a pipe cleaner, and push the other end through the hole, making the stamen and stem of each lily.

3. Draw and cut two identical paper stem-and-leaf sections for each lily. Make the stem wide enough for the pipe cleaner to fit onto. Place the pipe cleaner of each lily between the two leaf sections and glue together.

4. Place a small amount of clay in the bottom of a plastic-foam cup. Press the stems of the lilies into the clay. Add some tissue paper on top. Wrap the cup with aluminum foil, and add a bow.

ROCKY CHICK
(small paper plate, construction paper, markers)

1. Fold a small paper plate in half.

2. Draw and cut out two chicks the same size from construction paper. Glue the chicks together from their heads to the middle of their bodies.

3. Place the chicks on the fold of the paper plate so that half the chick is on each side. Glue in place.

4. Add features with markers. Stand the rocky chick toy on a table and make it rock.

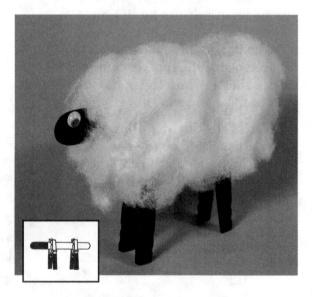

CLOTHESPIN LAMB
(two spring-type clothespins, ice-cream stick, cotton balls, moveable plastic eyes, poster paint)

1. Attach two spring-type clothespins to an ice-cream stick as shown. Paint the head and legs with black poster paint and let dry.

2. Glue cotton all over the lamb's body, leaving just the legs and head peeking out.

3. Glue moveable plastic eyes to each side of the lamb's head.

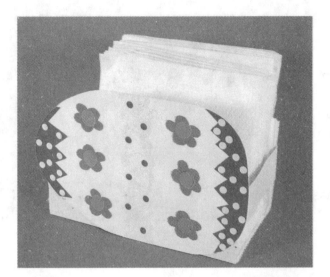

EGG NAPKIN HOLDER
(half-gallon milk carton, construction paper)

1. To make the holder, cut off the top, bottom, and one side of a half-gallon milk carton. Glue construction paper to the outside of the carton. Staple a strip of paper to each opened end of the carton.

2. Draw an egg shape on paper and decorate it. Cut it out, and glue it on one side of the carton. Place napkins inside the holder.

CONE BASKET
(ice-cream cone, plastic food wrap, ribbon)

1. Fill an empty ice-cream cone with assorted candies.

2. Cut a circle from plastic food wrap, and lay it over the top of the cone. Tie two ribbons around the top rim of the cone, and knot at opposite sides.

3. Bring the four ends of the ribbons up, and tie them together in a bow to make the handle. Hang the cone basket on someone's doorknob.

BUNNY IN A BASKET
(construction paper, yarn)

1. Fold a piece of construction paper in half. Cut out a basket about the size of your hand, using the fold as the bottom of the basket. Glue only the sides together.

2. Cut a paper handle for the basket, and glue the ends inside the basket. Decorate the front of the basket.

3. Make a bunny from two circles of paper. Add ears, eyes, and a nose from paper. Glue on yarn whiskers. Write an Easter message on the bunny's body, and slip the bunny inside the basket.

4. Cut a small gift tag from paper. On it write the name of the person the card is for and "Please pull out the bunny." Attach it to the handle of the basket with a piece of yarn.

NEST OF CHICKS

(plastic-foam trays, plastic grass, ribbon)

1. Cut chicks from plastic-foam trays. Add a ribbon bow around the neck of each chick and glue on paper-dot eyes.

2. Turn a plastic-foam tray over so the bottom is facing up. Make a slit where you want each chick to sit, using the point of a pencil or pen.

3. Place each chick in a slit with some glue. Brush glue around the chicks on the tray bottom. Press plastic grass into the glue and around the chicks. Let your decoration dry.

BUNNY BOOKHOLDER

(wire clothes hanger, one 2-inch and one 3-inch plastic-foam ball, construction paper, yarn)

1. Hold the top and bottom of a wire clothes hanger and pull. Bend up about 7 inches for the top and 5 inches for the bottom to form the shape for the base.

2. Decorate a 3-inch plastic-foam ball for the bunny head. Cut ears, eyes, and a nose from construction paper. Add a yarn mouth. Put the head on the 7-inch hanger section.

3. Use the 2-inch plastic-foam ball for the tail. Place it on the 5-inch hanger section. Place books between the head and the tail.

FOAM-TRAY NECKLACE

(plastic drinking straws, plastic-foam trays, string)

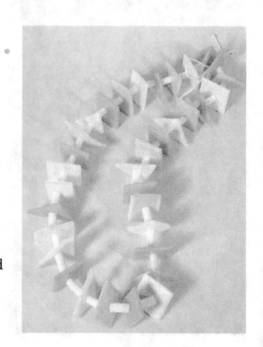

1. Cut shapes from different-colored plastic-foam trays.

2. Cut small pieces of plastic drinking straws.

3. Cut a piece of string long enough to go around your neck. Thread it onto a needle.

4. String a piece of plastic foam and then a section of straw onto the string. Continue with foam and straw until you have reached the end of the string.

5. Sew the end of the string through the first piece of plastic foam and knot the end, finishing the necklace.

LITTLE LAMB EASTER CARD
(construction paper, cotton balls, yarn)

1. Draw around your hand on a piece of black construction paper, and cut the shape out. The thumb is for the lamb's head, and the four fingers are for its legs.

2. Cover the rest of the body with cotton balls to look like wool. Add a paper dot for an eye. Cut and tie a piece of yarn around its neck.

3. Cut a small card from paper. Write a greeting on the card. Punch a hole in the card and one where the lamb's tail might be. Slip a piece of yarn through both holes and tie the ends.

STUFFED CHICKEN
(paper, felt, cotton balls, needle, thread)

1. Draw the outline of a chicken about 10 inches tall on paper. Place the pattern on a piece of felt and draw around it with a pencil. Do this again and cut out both chickens.

2. Place the two chickens together with the pencil lines on the inside. Sew them together around the edge, leaving a small section open.

3. Stuff cotton balls or pieces of scrap fabric inside the chicken through the small opening. Finish sewing, stuffing as you go.

4. Glue felt eyes and wings to the chicken.

DANCING BUNNIES
(construction paper)

1. Cut a piece of white paper 6 inches by 12 inches. Fold in half three times to 6 inches by 3 inches.

2. Draw and cut out half a bunny shape on the fold, but don't cut the ends of the arms.

3. Cut dresses, hair bows, slacks, suspenders, and bow ties from paper, and glue them to the bunnies. Add features with colored pens.

CUTOUT PAPER FAN
(paper, ribbon)

1. Use a sheet of paper about 8 1/2 inches by 11 inches. Fold it in accordion pleats, making the pleats 1/2 inch wide.

2. Holding the pleats together, turn one end over 1/2 inch and staple it together. Cut designs along the edges of the pleats about halfway down the pleats.

3. Tie a ribbon at the stapled end, and open the fan to see the design.

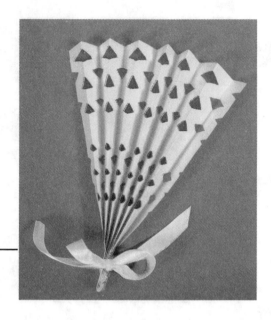

CHICKIE-IN-AN-EGG
(construction paper, plastic-foam cup, cotton balls, plastic drinking straw, plastic grass)

1. Glue or tape a piece of construction paper around a plastic-foam cup. Cut a jagged edge around the top of the cup to look like a broken eggshell.

2. Glue two cotton balls, one on top of the other, to the top of a drinking straw. Cut two eyes and a tiny beak from paper, and glue them to the chickie's head.

3. Glue plastic grass inside the cup. Use a pencil to poke a hole in the bottom of the cup. Push the end of the straw down through the hole, with the chickie in the cup.

4. Move the chickie in and out of its egg.

RABBIT-HEAD PUPPET
(cardboard egg carton, poster board, poster paint, construction paper, toothpicks, ribbon)

1. Cut one cup section from a cardboard egg carton. Cover it with white poster paint and let it dry.

2. To make the rabbit head, cut eyes, a nose, and a mouth from construction paper. Glue them to the bottom of the cup.

3. Paint six toothpicks for whiskers. Poke three holes on each side of the cup. Place the whiskers in the holes with glue.

4. Cut a small strip of poster board, and glue it to the back of the rabbit's head. Leave enough room so two fingers will fit inside. Glue a bow under his chin.

BOUQUET CARD

(construction paper, yarn, ribbon)

1. Fold a piece of white construction paper in half.

2. To make the flower buds, cut several 3 1/2-inch pieces of yarn. Spread circles of glue on the front of the card. Press a coil of yarn into each circle of glue. Glue a smaller coil of yarn on top of some of the flower buds.

3. Draw a stem and leaves for each flower bud. Add a ribbon bow to the bottom of the bouquet. Write a message inside the card.

BUNNY JUG BASKET

(one-gallon plastic jug, construction paper, ribbon, plastic grass)

1. Soak a one-gallon plastic jug in warm water to help soften it for cutting. Dry the jug. Draw the rabbit design at one end of the jug as shown in the picture. Cut along the lines.

2. To make the border, glue different-colored ribbon around the edge. Add features to the bunny's face with construction paper.

3. Fill the basket with plastic grass.

SHIMMERING JEWELRY

(large coffee can, coffee cup, poster board, paper, yarn)

1. Trace around a large coffee can on a piece of poster board. Do the same with a coffee cup.

2. Measure approximately 1/4 inch inside each line, and draw another line. Cut these circles along the lines, making two circular strips. One will be the necklace, the other, the bracelet.

3. Glue a piece of yarn to the back of each strip, leaving extra yarn at the ends.

4. Cut squares and circles from shiny, bright paper. Fold these shapes over the circular strips, and glue them in place.

5. Wear the jewelry by tying the ends of the yarn into bows.

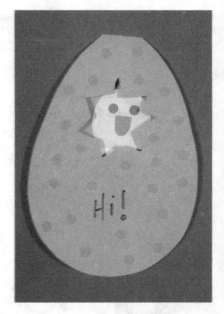

PEEKING-DUCK EASTER CARD

(construction paper)

1. Fold a piece of construction paper in half. Cut out an egg, keeping the top on the fold.

2. Open the egg and cut a jagged window out of the front. Close the egg and write "Hi!" under the window. Punch out paper dots and glue them around the window.

3. Cut out a circle of paper just large enough to fill the window. Glue on a paper beak and eyes, and glue the duck's head inside the card.

4. Write "Happy Easter" on a piece of paper and sign your name. Glue it to the front of the duck. Add paper wings and feet.

MILK CARTON EASTER BASKET

(half-gallon milk carton, construction paper)

1. To make the basket, cut a half-gallon milk carton in half.

2. For the handle, cut a 1-inch-wide section from the part that is leftover. Cut away one side of this section.

3. Cover the basket and handle with construction paper. Glue the handle to the basket. Decorate with cut-paper designs.

SMALL PUFFY PURSE

(felt, toothpick, shoestring)

1. Cut out a circle of felt 9 inches in diameter.

2. About 1 inch from the edge of the felt, draw twelve dots in the same positions as numbers on a clock.

3. Push a toothpick through each dot, and then thread a shoestring in and out of the holes.

4. Draw the ends of the shoestring together, and tie them in a tight bow.

FUZZY-WUZZY RABBIT PIN

(cardboard, cotton ball, moveable plastic eyes, construction paper, yarn, safety pin)

1. Cut a small circle from a piece of cardboard. Glue a cotton ball on top of the circle.

2. To make the rabbit's face, glue on two moveable plastic eyes and ears and whiskers made from construction paper.

3. Glue a small safety pin to the back of the cardboard. Attach the fuzzy-wuzzy rabbit to your shirt.

RABBIT MASK

(platter, poster board, construction paper, yarn)

1. Place a platter on a piece of poster board, and trace around the edge. Cut out the shape. Cut a slit from the edge to the center as shown. Pull one edge of the slit over the top of the other to form a small cone. Glue to hold it in place.

2. From construction paper, cut two large white circles and two smaller black circles for eyes and two triangle shapes for eyebrows. Glue them in place on the front of the mask.

3. Cut holes to see through in the center of each paper eye. Add ears, whiskers, and a mouth made from paper.

4. Poke a hole in each side of the mask and add yarn ties.

slits

THREE-D CHICK

(cardboard, bathroom tissue tube, poster paint)

1. Cut two identical chicks from cardboard. Cover them with poster paint and let them dry. Add eyes, beaks, and wings cut from painted cardboard.

2. Cut a 1-inch section from a bathroom tissue tube. Glue it between the two chicks.

LAMB PUPPET

(small brown paper bag, paper)

1. Draw and cut the lamb's head and ears from paper. Add eyes, a nose, and a mouth.

2. To make the lamb's curls, cut strips of paper and curl them by wrapping them around a pencil. Glue them between the lamb's ears. Glue the head to the bottom of the bag.

3. Cut the body from paper and glue it to the front of the bag. Add two paper feet.

4. Place your hand inside the bag, and curve your fingers over the fold to move the puppet's head.

FLUFFY RABBIT

(bathroom tissue tube, cotton, lightweight cardboard, construction paper)

1. To make the body, cut legs and feet from lightweight cardboard, and glue them to a bathroom tissue tube. Cover body, legs, and feet with glue and cotton.

2. Cut ears, eyes, whiskers, nose, and mouth from construction paper. Glue them to the bunny body. Add a large cotton ball for the tail.

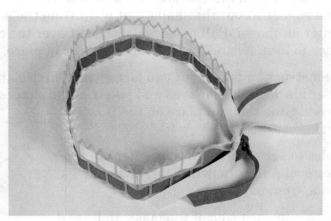

BERRY-BASKET RIBBON BELT

(two plastic berry baskets, ribbon)

1. Cut the bottoms from two plastic berry baskets and throw them away. Then cut through the corner of each side section, making a total of eight sections. (Because there are different basket designs, you may have a different pattern than shown.)

2. Weave two pieces of ribbon, each a yard long, in and out through the holes, adding new sections of the baskets as you need them.

3. When the belt fits your waist, tie the ends of the ribbons, and your belt will be finished.

EASTER BASKET SURPRISE

(two plastic-foam cups, paper doily, pipe cleaner, ribbon, construction paper, plastic grass)

1. Place a saucer on a piece of construction paper and draw around it. Cut out the circle and glue a paper doily on top.

2. Cut about 1 1/2 inches from the bottom of one plastic-foam cup. Turn another plastic-foam cup upside down and glue the first cup on top. Tie a ribbon around the center where the cups join.

3. Punch a hole in each side of the top cup. Insert a pipe cleaner for the handle, twisting the ends to hold it in place. Add a ribbon. Fill the top with plastic grass and a treat.

4. Place the basket on the paper doily at each table setting. Place a small candy rabbit or candy egg in the center of the doily, and put the basket over it.

5. When the guests pick up their baskets, they will find the surprise underneath.

EASTER MOBILE

(construction paper, toothpicks, four buttons, string)

1. Following the photo, cut two of each shape from construction paper.

2. Glue two ear pieces back to back. Then glue the other two ear pieces together. Insert the ears between the two top-of-head sections, and glue the head pieces together.

3. Glue the eye pieces together in pairs. Do the same with the chin sections. For whiskers, color six toothpicks and insert them between the nose pieces, and glue the nose in place.

4. Punch small holes and insert strings to assemble the pieces of the mobile as shown. Glue a small button to each side of both eye pieces. Add a string hanger.

CHICK NAPKIN RING

(poster board, poster paint, paper napkin)

1. Draw and cut a chick from a piece of poster board. Add an eye and beak using poster paint.

2. Draw and cut out a circle from the middle of the chick.

3. Insert a paper napkin through the hole. Place one chick with a napkin for each guest at the dinner table.

Eggs, Eggs, and More Eggs...

HOW TO MAKE A HARD-BOILED EGG
(whole raw egg, saucepan, water, stove)

1. Have an adult help you use the stove. Fill a saucepan halfway with cool water. Place the egg in the pan and bring the water to a slow boil, using low heat.

2. Cook the egg for seven minutes from the boiling point. Remove the pan from the heat and let the egg cool.

HOW TO BLOW OUT THE INSIDE OF A RAW EGG
(whole raw egg, large sewing needle)

1. Stick a large sewing needle into the pointed end of a raw egg, making sure to poke through the membrane under the shell. Turn the egg over, and stick the needle through the other end, making a larger hole than the first.

2. Over a large bowl, blow through the small hole, allowing the inside of the egg to flow into the bowl. Carefully rinse the shell in cold water.

HOW TO DYE EGGS WITH FOOD COLORING
(blown or hard-boiled eggs, food coloring, coffee mug, a teaspoon, white vinegar)

1. Add one teaspoon of white vinegar to one cup of hot water from the kitchen tap. Place several drops of food coloring into the hot water.

2. Place an egg in the mixture. Hold the egg down gently in the mixture with a spoon.

3. When the egg reaches the color you want, remove it and let it dry on a paper towel.

COLOR CHART	
To make:	**Combine:**
LIME GREEN	1 drop green + 3 drops yellow
ORANGE	2 drops red + 3 drops yellow
TURQUOISE	1 drop green + 4 drops blue
VIOLET	2 drops red + 2 drops blue
Experiment on your own to find other colors.	

EGG HEAD
(hard-boiled egg, permanent markers, yarn)

1. Sketch features on a hard-boiled egg. Color them with permanent markers.

2. Add glue and yarn for hair.

POLKA-DOT EGG
(hard-boiled egg, construction paper)

Using a paper punch, punch many different-colored dots from construction paper. Glue them to a hard-boiled egg.

EGG ANIMAL
(blown egg, pipe cleaner, cardboard egg carton, construction paper)

1. To make a piglet, cut and glue construction-paper features on a brown egg. Glue on a small piece of pipe cleaner for the tail.

2. Cut a cup section from a cardboard egg carton, and paint it with poster paints for the pig's feet. Glue the egg to the feet.

YARN GIFT EGG
(blown egg, yarn)

1. Draw a design on an egg lightly with a pencil. Trace over a small section of the design with glue.

2. Place yarn in the glue. Continue until you have covered the design with yarn.

WHITE-CRAYON SURPRISE EGG
(hard-boiled egg, white crayon)

1. Before you dye some eggs, draw designs on white eggs with a white crayon. Any areas of the egg covered with the white crayon will not take the color of the dye.

2. After you have dyed the egg, you will see your design appear.

KALEIDOSCOPE EGG
(blown egg, old magazine, clear nail polish)

1. Cut small squares of several colors from old magazine pages. Glue the squares on the eggshell, overlapping each square until the egg is covered.

2. After the squares are dry, paint the egg with one or two coats of clear nail polish.

RABBIT PLACE CARD
(poster board, cotton ball, construction paper,
yarn, paper doily)

1. Fold a small piece of poster board in half. Glue on a cotton ball for the rabbit's head.

2. Add pieces cut from a paper doily, construction paper, and yarn to create the rabbit's features.

3. Write a dinner guest's name on the card.

HATCH A CHICK
(hard-boiled egg, poster board)

1. Use a hard-boiled egg for the body of the chick.

2. On a folded piece of poster board, draw and cut out a tail and a head and neck as shown. The part that touches the fold should not be cut.

3. Glue the neck to the egg, leaving the feather ends free. Glue the tail in place.

4. Cut small teardrop-shaped feathers from poster board. Glue only the pointed end of each feather to the egg, inserting each one under the neck feathers and so on down the body. No feathers are needed on the bottom.

5. After the glue has dried, carefully bend out each feather, and you'll find the chick can stand without tipping over.

GIFT WRAP HAT
(gift wrap, yarn, tissue paper)

1. Cut two 20-inch circles from gift wrap. Glue them back to back so the pattern shows on both sides.

2. While the circle is still damp from the glue, put it on your head. Look in the mirror as you mold the center of the circle to fit the shape of your head (or have someone help you).

3. Leave the edges of the circle sticking out all around as a brim. Tie a piece of yarn around the hat where the brim begins.

4. Remove the yarn when the hat is dry. Make a tissue paper bow, and glue it to the hat.

MAGNETIC BUNNY

(plastic-foam egg carton, paper, felt,
magnetic strip, broom straw)

1. Cut two egg cups from a plastic-foam egg carton.

2. To make the rabbit shape, draw circles that are larger than an egg cup on a piece of heavy paper. Add ears and feet. Cut out the paper rabbit pattern.

3. Place the pattern on a piece of felt, and trace around it with a pencil. Cut out the felt rabbit.

4. Glue the two egg cups on the rabbit. Add features from felt and whiskers from broom straw. Glue a magnetic strip to the back of the rabbit.

5. Place your rabbit on the refrigerator door for the holiday.

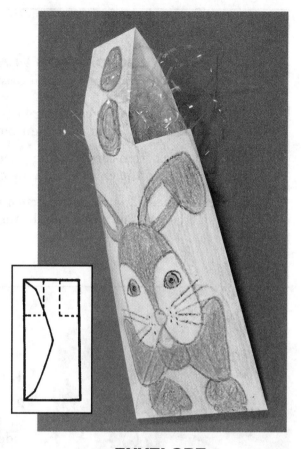

ENVELOPE EASTER BASKET

(unused envelope, crayons, plastic grass)

1. Moisten the flap of an unused long white envelope and seal it shut. Cut out two sections of the envelope as shown.

2. Decorate the basket with drawings made with crayons. Fill the basket with plastic grass.

BUTTON PIN

(buttons, felt, embroidery needle,
embroidery floss, cardboard, safety pin)

1. Cut a small strip of felt. Using embroidery floss and a needle, sew some buttons on the felt.

2. Glue the piece of felt with the buttons on a piece of cardboard and let dry.

3. Trim the edges with scissors to look like leaves. Glue a safety pin to the back.

EGG-CARTON PLACE CARD

(cardboard egg carton, construction paper)

1. Cut two cups from a cardboard egg carton for each place card. Glue the two cups with their bottoms together.

2. Cut a chick from construction paper. Add features with paper, and glue the chick inside the cup.

3. Print a guest's name on a piece of paper, and glue it to the front of the cup. Put a few jelly beans inside.

BUNNY CARD

(construction paper, cotton ball)

1. Draw a bunny on white construction paper and cut it out.

2. Glue the bunny to the inside of a piece of folded paper so that half is on one side of the fold and half is on the other side. Add paper ears and write a message.

3. Make the spring by cutting two strips of paper and folding as shown. Glue the spring between the two halves of the card.

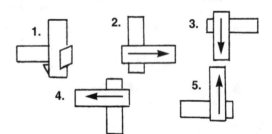

4. Write a greeting on the front of the card.

EASTER EGGCUP

(cardboard egg carton, poster paint, construction paper)

1. To make a special cup for Easter eggs, cut two cup sections from a cardboard egg carton.

2. Trim one top evenly for the base. Trim the other one to look like flower petals. Glue the two cups with their bottoms together.

3. Cover the cups with poster paint. When dry decorate with paper-punch dots.

RABBIT'S RING-TOSS GAME

(paper towel tube, cardboard, poster paint, rubber bands, poster board)

1. Cut a head, front feet, and back feet for the rabbit from a piece of cardboard. Paint them white and let dry. Add details with paint and markers.

2. For the body of the rabbit, paint a paper towel tube white and let dry. Cut two vertical slits almost in the middle of the tube. Insert the front feet through the slits.

3. Glue the head and the back feet to the body. Hold in place with rubber bands until dry. Glue the rabbit to a square cardboard base.

4. Cut strips of poster board, and tape them together to form rings. Make up a point system for the game. For example, a ring on an ear might be worth 10 points and one on a paw, 15 points.

JELLY-BEAN BASKET

(small margarine container, construction paper, poster board, brass fasteners, plastic grass)

1. Use a small margarine container for the basket.

2. For the handle, cut a strip of poster board, and punch a hole at each end. Punch a hole at opposite sides of the basket. Fasten the handle to the basket with brass fasteners.

3. Decorate the basket with cut-paper flowers. Add some plastic grass and jelly beans.

FLOWER HAT

(6-inch paper plate, poster paint, construction paper, ribbon)

1. For the center of the flower, paint the back of a 6-inch paper plate with poster paint and let dry.

2. From construction paper, cut six flower-shaped petals about 6 inches long. Glue these around the edge of the plate.

3. Cut and glue two leaves between two of the petals on opposite sides of the plate.

4. Punch a hole on opposite sides of the plate, going through a leaf on each side. Thread a piece of long ribbon through the holes with the ribbon on top of the flower center. Tie the ribbon in a bow under your chin.

CHICK EASTER CARD
(construction paper)

1. On a piece of folded white paper, draw a chick with its back on the fold. Cut it out. Color the chick's front yellow, its eye black, and its beak orange.

2. Fold a piece of construction paper for a card. Glue the chick to the front of the card.

3. Cut out and glue on tail feathers of various colors. Cut one wing on a fold of yellow paper, and glue it to the chick. Add legs and feet with a marker.

4. Outline the edge of the inside of the chick with yellow marker. Write "Easter Greetings" on the inside of the chick. Write a message inside the card.

TULIP WREATH
(sixteen ice-cream sticks, poster paint, construction paper)

1. Paint sixteen ice-cream sticks with poster paint, and let them dry thoroughly.

2. Glue two of the sticks together at the center so they form a skinny X. Continue to form X's with the remaining sticks.

3. Make the wreath by arranging the X's in a circle and gluing them together, end to end.

4. Cut and glue construction-paper tulips and leaves. Make a bow from tissue paper, and glue it to the wreath.

BUNNY BASKET
(milk carton, poster board, cotton, felt, construction paper)

1. For the basket, cut away the top portion of the milk carton.

2. Cut two ears from poster board, and glue them to the basket.

3. Cover the base and ears with glue and cotton.

4. Add eyes, a nose, and a mouth cut from felt. Cut paper features for the ears.

5. Cut a strip of construction paper for the handle, and glue it to the basket.

GIFT WRAP TIE
(gift wrap, poster board, shoestring)

1. Glue gift wrap to both sides of a strip of poster board. Cut the poster board in the shape of a man's necktie.

2. Glue the knot end of the tie to the middle of a shoestring. Cover the string with some of the gift wrap.

3. Cut out a white paper bunny, and glue it to the front of the tie.

4. To wear the tie, place the shoestring under your shirt collar. Tie the ends together in a bow.

MISTER RABBIT
(washcloth, safety pin, needle, heavy thread, cotton)

1. Roll in two sides of a washcloth tightly to the center. Pin in the middle with a safety pin.

2. To make the ears, hold the rolled sides down and push the cloth down between the rolls halfway to the pin. Tie each ear at the base with heavy thread.

3. Tie the cloth in the middle to form the head, and remove the pin. Open out the head, stuff with cotton, and sew shut.

4. For the legs, open the rolled ends slightly, tuck a thin layer of cotton up into each side, and roll tightly again. With the rolled side down, push up the cloth between the rolls to the "tummy" and sew it to the legs.

5. Open the body and stuff with cotton. Sew up the back. Add features to the rabbit's face with felt. Use thread for the whiskers. Add a felt bow under his chin.

6. Cut a coat from felt and sew up the sides. Stuff cotton-ball hands in the sleeves, and sew in place. Dress the rabbit in his coat. Sew on a cotton ball for the tail. Add a felt scarf.

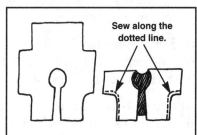

Sew along the dotted line.

EGG-SHELL CUP

(white egg shells, rolling pin, wooden board, poster paint, construction paper, small cardboard container)

1. Wash white egg shells and remove the thin skin from the inside. Let them dry for several days. Place the shells on a wooden board. With a rolling pin, crush them into fine pieces, but not powder.

2. Mix white poster paint with glue until the mixture is like yogurt and has a nice white color.

3. Glue a construction paper handle to the outer sides of a small cardboard container. Cover the handle ends and the container with construction paper.

4. Using the glue-paint mixture, paint a design on the container. Sprinkle the crushed eggshells over the design. The eggshells will stick to the mixture, giving the design a delicate, lacy look.

EGG-CARTON BASKET

(plastic-foam egg cartons, pipe cleaner, paper, plastic grass)

1. For the base of the basket, cut out the center section of a plastic-foam egg carton containing four cups.

2. For the flowers, cut out egg cups from another carton of a different color and poke two holes, opposite each other, in the cup bottom.

3. For the handle, poke a hole at opposite sides of the carton. Push a long pipe cleaner into one hole and twist the end. Thread the flowers onto the pipe cleaner, and push the end into the other hole on the carton and twist the end. Add paper leaves.

BOX BUNNY

(cardboard cookie box, heavy white paper, 6-inch paper plates, white tissue paper)

1. Secure the ends of a cardboard cookie box with tape. Wrap the box with heavy white paper.

2. Cut strips of 2-inch-wide white tissue paper. Fold the strips and fringe them by cutting 1-inch slits about 1/4 inch apart. Glue the strips to the sides of the box, beginning at the bottom and overlapping each new strip.

3. For the bunny head, glue short strips of fringe around the edge of a 6-inch paper plate. Cut the ears from another paper plate, and glue them to the back of the first paper plate.

4. Cut a 4-inch-round circle from heavy white paper for the bunny face. Add features with markers. Glue the face in the center of the head. Glue the head to the body of the bunny.

41

SEE-THROUGH EASTER CARD
(construction paper, plastic food wrap, permanent markers)

1. For each card, place two sheets of 9-by-12-inch construction paper on top of each other. On the 12-inch side of each sheet, draw a vertical line at 4 inches and at 8 inches, dividing the sheets into three panels.

2. Cut a tulip design from the center of another piece of paper measuring 4-by-9 inches. Using this as a stencil, trace the design on each panel and cut out the tulip.

3. Spread glue around the edges of the paper and the tulip design. Place a piece of plastic food wrap on top. Spread glue around the edges of the food wrap. Place the other piece of paper on top of this. Press together.

4. Using a marker, color one area of the plastic-wrap tulip design on one panel only. Use another marker and color another area of the design on another panel of plastic wrap. Then color the last panel with a third marker. Fold the outside panels over the center panel so the designs overlap.

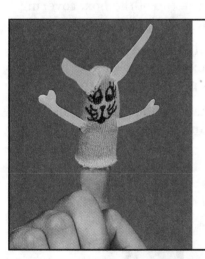

GLOVE FINGER PUPPET
(old cotton glove, fine-line permanent marker, heavy white paper)

1. Cut off the finger of an old glove. Draw a face on the tip of the finger with a fine-line permanent marker.

2. From heavy white paper, cut out rabbit ears and paws. Cut tiny slits in the glove finger, and glue the ears and paws in place.

EASTER RABBIT HAT
(construction paper, moveable plastic eyes)

1. Draw and cut out a pattern of two bunny heads and a headband as shown. Fold an 18-by-12-inch sheet of construction paper in half.

2. Place the pattern with the heads on the fold, and trace around the pattern.

3. Cut out the bunnies and the headband up to the fold, which should be left uncut.

4. Unfold and decorate the bunnies with markers, and add moveable plastic eyes. Cut the headband strip to fit around your head, and glue the ends together.

RICKRACK NOTE CARD
(construction paper, rickrack)

1. Fold a piece of construction paper in half to form a card.

2. Cut small pieces of rickrack and glue them to the front of the card. With a marker decorate them to look like chicks.

3. Add other details to the card with more rickrack, paper, and markers. Write a message inside.

FLOWER-BOX MOBILE
(four small gelatin boxes, one large box, construction paper, yarn)

1. Cover a large box with glue and construction paper. Poke two holes, one opposite the other, in the middle of the narrow sides of the box. Glue the ends of a piece of yarn into each hole to form a hanger. Glue a strip of paper around the top of the box, covering the yarn on each side, to help hold the yarn hanger in place.

2. Cover four small gelatin boxes with glue and paper. Create paper flowers and glue them to the boxes. With a pencil, poke a hole in the top of each box and glue a piece of yarn into each hole.

3. Poke four holes in the bottom of the large box. Insert the yarn ends from the four small boxes and glue them in place. After the glue has dried, hang the mobile.

CROSS FOR EASTER
(poster board, white tissue paper, old newspaper, plastic spray bottle, water, food coloring, string)

1. Draw and cut out a cross from a piece of poster board. Cut out small shapes using scissors and a paper punch.

2. Place sheets of old newspaper on your work surface. Lay white tissue, larger than the cross, on top of the newspaper.

3. Fill a spray bottle with water and moisten the tissue paper with a fine mist, making it damp, not wet. Sprinkle drops of food coloring on the tissue paper and let dry.

4. Put a thin layer of glue on one side of the cross and lay it on the tissue paper. Trim the edges. Punch a hole at the top and attach a string hanger.

5. Hang the cross in a window.

WOVEN BASKET
(9-inch paper plate, 18-by-12-inch construction paper)

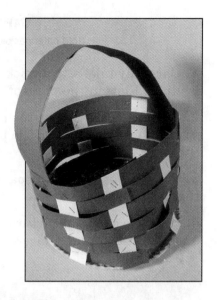

1. Cut eight strips of white construction paper, each 9 inches long and 1 inch wide. Staple the ends of the strips to the bottom edge of a 9-inch paper plate at equal distances apart. Bend the strips upward at the edge of the plate.

2. Cut strips of brown construction paper, each 18 inches long and 1 inch wide. Staple two strips together and weave in and out through the white strips. Cut off the excess. Staple where each vertical strip crosses a horizontal strip.

3. Continue weaving until you reach the top of the white strips or stop and cut off the excess. Cut two 2-inch-wide strips for the handle and glue together. Staple the ends to the basket.

FELT BOARD EGG HUNT
(corrugated cardboard, felt)

1. Cut a piece of cardboard to measure 18 inches by 12 inches. Spread glue on one side, and cover it with a piece of felt. Trim the edges with scissors, or tape them to the back.

2. To make the picture, cut pieces of felt in the shape of a rabbit, a basket, a chick, a tree, clouds, a stone wall—or other items—and place them on the felt board.

3. Cut out small felt eggs. Hide them behind the felt objects in your picture.

4. Let your friends take turns searching behind the felt objects for the eggs. Change the picture over and over.

TUBE RABBIT
(bathroom tissue tube, poster paint, heavy white paper, construction paper, cotton ball)

1. Paint a bathroom tissue tube with poster paint and let dry. Cut front and back legs, ears, and a circle from heavy white paper. Paint them and let dry.

2. Place the tube end on the circle and draw around the outside. Cut out the circle. This will be the head.

3. Glue the head, with the ears in between, at one end of the tube. Glue the legs on each side of the tube. Add a cotton-ball tail.

4. Cut out paper features, and glue them to the rabbit head.

GIFT BOX
(old calendar picture, toothpick box)

1. Carefully take a toothpick box apart at the places where it is glued. Flatten the piece of cardboard.

2. Lay the cardboard on the back of an old calendar picture, so an interesting part of the picture will appear on the top of the box.

3. Trace around the cardboard edge with a pencil, and cut out the shape with scissors.

4. Glue the calendar picture to the cardboard. Fold the box and glue it together. Place a small gift inside.

GLITTER EGG MOBILE
(white poster board, glitter, string)

1. Cut a basket from an 8-inch-square piece of white poster board. Cut four eggs from poster board.

2. Squeeze glue on the basket and the eggs, creating designs. Sprinkle on glitter and let dry. Do the same on the other side.

3. Punch one hole at the top of the basket and a hole at the bottom for each egg. Punch a hole at the top of each egg.

4. Attach the eggs with pieces of string. Make a loop hanger at the top of the basket.

SEED-FLOWER BOUQUET
(poster board, pipe cleaner, pumpkin seeds, round food container, clay, fabric)

1. For each flower, cut a 1-inch circle from a piece of poster board. With a pen, poke two small holes in the center of each circle.

2. Insert one end of a pipe cleaner through the holes and wrap it around the stem underneath the circle. Glue pumpkin seeds on the top of the circle to create flower petals.

3. Loop short pieces of pipe cleaner and twist them onto the stems for leaves.

4. Press clay into a round food container to hold the stems in place.

5. Cover the outside of the container with glue and fabric.

PAPER BASKET
(construction paper)

1. With a ruler and a pencil, mark a 9-by-12-inch piece of construction paper as shown.

2. Cut on the solid lines. Cut little holes in the larger sections. Fold on all the dotted lines as shown.

3. Glue the bottom flaps in place and join the sides of the basket at the fold. Cut out a long narrow strip of paper, and glue it to the basket for the handle.

4. Decorate the sides with cutout pieces of paper.

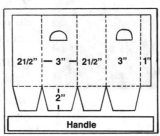

BUNNY BOX
(bathroom tissue tube, half-gallon milk carton, construction paper, plastic grass, cotton ball)

1. To make the basket, cut a half-gallon milk carton so that a 2-inch-high box is left. Cover the basket with construction paper.

2. To make the head, cover a bathroom tissue tube with construction paper. Decorate with cut-paper features for the bunny's face.

3. Cut out bunny ears. Glue the ears between the basket and the bunny's head. Hold together with paper clips until the glue is dry. Add plastic grass and a cotton-ball tail.

COTTON-BALL CHICK
(poster board, cotton balls, paper)

1. From poster board, cut the body base and feet as shown.

2. Glue the feet to the body base. Cover them with cotton balls glued together to form the body of a chick.

3. From paper, cut and glue a beak and eyes to the chick.

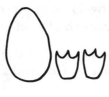

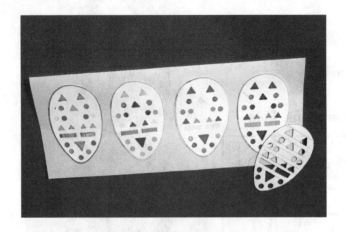

STENCIL EGG CARD

(heavy white paper, construction paper, permanent markers,
paper punch)

1. Fold a piece of construction paper in half to make a card.

2. Cut an egg shape from heavy white paper. Cut small shapes from the egg with a paper punch and scissors to make a stencil.

3. Place the egg stencil on white paper. Color around the egg and in the holes with permanent markers. Cut out the eggs and glue them to the outside of the card. Write a message inside the card.

CANDLE CENTERPIECE

(bathroom tissue tube, 6-inch paper plate, glitter, construction paper)

1. Spread glue around the rim of a 6-inch paper plate. Sprinkle some glitter on the glue. Let dry and shake off the loose glitter.

2. Cover a bathroom tissue tube with paper. Dip one end of the tube in glue, and place it in the center of the paper plate. Let dry. Add a paper flame.

3. Cut leaves and colorful flower petals from paper. Glue them around the candle. Wad up a piece of paper, and glue it in the center of the flower.

FLOWER BASKET

(half-gallon milk carton, construction paper, white poster board,
margarine tub)

1. Measure 3 1/2 inches from the bottom of a half-gallon milk carton. Cut off the top and cover the bottom with construction paper to make a flower pot.

2. From white poster board, cut two 5-by-11-inch pieces. Cut a slot for a handle about 3/4 of an inch from the top of each piece.

3. Glue paper the same color as the bottom half of the carton to the bottom of the white poster board pieces. Cut and glue on a paper flower.

4. Glue the poster board pieces on opposite sides of the carton, joining the handle at the top. Hold in place with spring-type clothespins until dry. Place a small flower plant in a margarine tub and put it inside the basket.

BOBBIN' HEAD BUNNY

(gelatin box, small stones, construction paper, heavy paper, pipe cleaner, cotton ball)

1. To make the bunny body, place small stones inside a gelatin box and tape the flaps shut. Cover the box with construction paper.

2. To make the bunny head, cut two circles and four ears from construction paper. Cut one circle and two ears from heavier paper. These must all be the same size.

3. To assemble, glue the construction-paper ears to each side of the heavier-paper ears. Glue the construction-paper circles to each side of the heavier-paper circle, inserting the ears and the end of a 5-inch pipe cleaner in between. Hold all in place with paper clips until dry. Add paper features.

4. Coil up the other end of the pipe cleaner and glue it to the body. Cut out four legs and glue them to the sides. Add a cotton ball for the tail.

5. Tap the bunny head and watch it bob back and forth.

SPOOL NECKLACE

(empty thread spools, gift wrap paper, paper punch, yarn)

1. Cut and glue strips of gift wrap paper around empty thread spools of various sizes.

2. Place the spool ends on the gift wrap paper and trace around them with a pencil. Cut out the circles of paper and glue them on the spool ends. Push a pencil point through the center hole.

3. Thread the spools on a piece of yarn long enough to go loosely around your neck. Tie a bow at the ends.

EASTER BONNET CUP

(paper doily, construction paper, ribbon, plastic grass)

1. Cut a 2 1/2-inch circle from the center of an 8-inch-round paper doily. Cut the doily as shown, creating tabs around the circle. Bend the tabs upward.

2. Cut a 6-inch circle of construction paper, and glue the paper doily in the center with the tabs bent upward.

3. Cut a strip of construction paper 2 inches by 9 inches long. Wrap the strip around the tabs in the doily. Glue the tabs to the inside of the strip. Glue the ends of the strip together.

4. Decorate with pieces of cut paper doily and ribbon. Fill the cup with plastic grass and treats.

BUNNY CARD
(construction paper, two tongue depressors, poster paint, gift wrap)

1. Fold a 10-by-12-inch piece of construction paper in half.

2. Paint two tongue depressors with white poster paint. They will need two coats of paint to cover completely.

3. Glue the depressors on the front of the card for the bunny's ears. Cut a circle from construction paper for the bunny's head.

4. Cut a tie from gift wrap, and glue it in place. Draw a face with a marker. Write a message inside.

EGG CHAIN
(heavy white paper, markers, ribbon)

1. Cut out eggs from heavy white paper. The more eggs, the longer the chain will be.

2. In the middle of each egg, cut two vertical slits. Using markers, draw designs on the eggs.

3. Form the chain by weaving a long piece of ribbon through the slits in each egg.

RABBIT AND CHICK BOX
(aluminum foil box, construction paper, poster board, plastic grass)

1. With scissors, cut the metal edge from the front of an aluminum foil box. Cover the sides and the front of the box with construction paper. Tape to hold in place.

2. Trim off the top lid edge and cut seven tabs as shown.

3. Draw and cut out rabbits and chicks from poster board. Decorate with markers. Glue them to the front of the tabs.

4. Fill the box with plastic grass and wait for Peter Cottontail.

Box top

Back of box

FANCY PHOTO FRAME

(lightweight cardboard, gift wrap, white paper, poster paint)

1. Cut two identical rectangular pieces of lightweight cardboard, one for the back section and one for the front section. From the front section, cut out an area large enough to fit a photo.

2. Cover one side of each cardboard with gift wrap and tape the edges on the back. To help fit the paper around the cutout section, cut an X from corner to corner, fold the paper back, and secure with tape.

3. Place a photo in the opening, and tape it to the back of the front section. Glue the two sections together around the edges.

4. Cut a small piece of cardboard, and cover it with paper. Tape it to the middle of the back of the frame to help make it stand up.

5. Draw and cut out eggs, rabbits, and chicks from white paper and decorate. Glue them around the picture frame.

BUTTON FLOWERS

(white poster board, lightweight fabric, pipe cleaners, large flat two-hole buttons)

1. Insert a pipe cleaner through one hole in a large, flat button and back through the other hole. Twist the ends together under the button to make a stem.

2. Spread glue on a piece of white poster board and press a piece of lightweight fabric on top. Let dry.

3. Cut out several fabric petals, and glue them to the underside of the button.

4. Bend short pieces of pipe cleaner into leaf shapes, and twist them onto the stem.

FLOWER BLOSSOM PICTURE

(construction paper, poster board, plastic-foam egg cartons)

1. For the background of your picture, glue a piece of blue construction paper to a piece of poster board.

2. Cut out stems and leaves from green paper, and glue to the background.

3. Cut out plastic-foam egg carton cups. With scissors, trim the cups to look like flowers. Glue them to the stems.

4. Add a paper butterfly in the sky.

SHINY EASTER CARD
(heavy white paper, gift wrap)

1. Fold a piece of heavy white paper in half to make a card.

2. Cut a scalloped edge at the bottom of the front of the card. Glue a strip of shiny gift wrap, on the inside bottom of the back half of the card.

3. Cut flowers from the same shiny gift wrap and glue them to the front of the card. Add stems and leaves with a marker.

HANGING EASTER BASKET
(construction paper, ribbon, cardboard, silk or dried flowers)

1. Fold a square piece of construction paper as shown in A. At the top point, draw a circle the size of a doorknob and cut it out as shown in B.

2. Fold up the bottom point of the paper to meet the top edge as shown in C, and staple to hold the basket shape. Glue a ribbon bow on top of the staple.

3. To reinforce the hole, cut a hole in a square piece of cardboard to match the size of the hole in the paper. Glue the cardboard hole to the back of the paper directly behind the hole.

4. Fill the basket with silk or dried flowers and hang it on a doorknob as a gift.

RABBIT WITH BUILT-IN EARS
(cardboard egg carton, bathroom tissue tube, poster paint, gift wrap, felt, paper, ribbon, cotton ball)

1. Cut a four-cup section from a cardboard egg carton for the base. Trim evenly around the cups with scissors. Cover the section with poster paint.

2. Paint an ice-cream stick and let dry. Push the ice-cream stick through the middle of the cone-shaped divider to create arms.

3. Look carefully at a bathroom tissue tube. You will see that at each end the cardboard ends in a point. Pry the points up and peel them back to form ears. Paint the tube inside and out.

4. Cut 1-inch-deep fringes around the tube ends. Bend the fringes out. Add pieces of felt and paper for the rabbit's face and gift wrap for the ears.

5. Make a neck hole about the size of a dime in the bottom of the tube. Spread glue around the cone top in the center of the four-cup section, and place the tube on top, above the arms. Let dry. Tie a ribbon around the rabbit's neck. Add a cotton ball for a tail.

EGG DOLL

(blown egg, bathroom tissue tube, paper baking cups, paper, ribbon, permanent marker)

1. Blow out an egg, following the directions on page 32, and set it aside.

2. Use a bathroom tissue tube for the body. Cut out the bottoms from paper baking cups, and slip them over the tube for the dress. Add tape if needed.

3. Glue the egg to the top of the tube and let dry. Draw a face with a permanent marker.

4. Tie a ribbon around the doll's neck. Fold a baking cup to look like a bonnet, and glue it to the doll's head. Add cut-paper flowers.

FRINGE FLOWERS

(poster board, burlap, string)

1. Cut simple shapes for grass and flowers from a loosely woven fabric like burlap.

2. Pull the threads carefully, one by one, from one or more edges of the shape to give a "fringed" look.

3. Glue the shapes on a piece of poster board. Add a string to the back for a hanger.

BUNNY CRAYON FUZZIES

(construction paper, heavy paper, crayons, string)

1. Draw rabbit shapes on heavy paper, and cut them out to use as patterns.

2. Place the rabbit pattern on a piece of construction paper. Starting in about a 1/2 inch on the pattern, stroke a crayon over the edge and onto the paper. Use zigzag, curly, or straight strokes for different effects.

3. Remove the pattern and add other features with crayons or markers.

4. Glue your picture to a large piece of heavy paper for a frame. Add a string hanger.

EASTER EGG-HUNT CARD
(construction paper, plastic grass)

1. For the card, cut a 6-by-9-inch piece of construction paper. Fold it in half. On the front write, "Look for the hidden Easter message inside."

2. Draw several eggs on white paper. Draw one egg with a 1-inch tab at the bottom.

3. Cut out the eggs, and color them with markers. Write your message on the back of the egg that has the tab.

4. On the bottom of the inside of the card, spread glue and press plastic grass for a nest. Glue the eggs in place, but leave an unglued space in which to slip the tabbed egg.

5. The receiver of the card will need to hunt for the message.

LACY BASKET
(paper cup, paper doily, pipe cleaner, ribbon)

1. Place a cup upside down in the center of a round paper doily and trace around it.

2. Poke a hole in the center of the doily and cut to the circle you have traced.

3. Make eight cuts as shown, going to different points on the circle.

4. Place the cup upright on the center of the doily and push the doily up to the rim of the cup. Add a little glue.

5. Poke a hole in each side of the cup, and push a pipe cleaner through the holes to make a handle. Add bows made from ribbon.

EASTER TREE
(construction paper, fabric, plastic-foam cup, clay, fallen tree branch, thread, yarn)

1. Place a fallen tree branch into a plastic-foam cup filled with clay. Cut out a circle of fabric about 12 inches in diameter. Place the cup in the center, and gather the fabric around the base of the branch. Tie a piece of yarn to hold the fabric in place.

2. Cut out lots of paper eggs. Decorate them with markers. Punch a hole through the top of each egg. String a short piece of thread through each hole, and tie the other end to a twig.

FLOATING WATER LILIES

(large glass or ceramic bowl, water, food coloring, plastic-foam egg cartons)

1. For each flower, scallop the edges of two cups cut from a plastic-foam egg carton. Glue one inside another.

2. Cut leaves from the flat part of the carton. Glue the flower on top.

3. Fill a bowl with water colored with blue food coloring in the kitchen sink. Float the lilies on the water.

4. Have an adult help you place the bowl in the center of the dining room table.

BUTTON-BUNNY PLACE CARD

(poster board, buttons, permanent marker)

1. Fold a 4-inch-square piece of poster board in half.

2. Glue a large smooth-top button on the left side of the card, near the bottom, for the bunny's body.

3. Glue a small two-hole button above the large button. With a marker, darken in the small button holes for eyes. Add other features. Cut pieces of thread, and glue them in place for whiskers.

4. Print the name of your guest on the place card.

DOUGH BEADS

(white bread, white glue, acrylic paint, plastic bags, waxed paper, rolling pin, toothpick, needle and heavy thread, button)

1. Remove the crust from a slice of bread, and tear the bread into small pieces in a bowl. Add a tablespoon of white glue and drops of acrylic paint, and mix it all together.

2. Knead by working the dough in your hands and on a flat surface until it's smooth and elastic.

3. Use a rolling pin to roll the dough out onto a sheet of waxed paper. Form the dough into small balls and circles. Let them dry for an hour. Then make a hole in each with a toothpick. Let them dry for a day.

4. With a needle, string the beads on a heavy piece of doubled thread. After you have finished, tie a knot at one end of the thread. Tie a button at the other end. Place the button in the loop to fasten the beads around your neck.

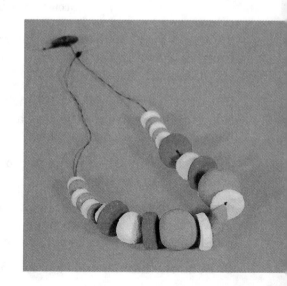

HAPPY EASTER FAN
(five ice-cream sticks, construction paper, ribbon)

1. Arrange five ice-cream sticks in a fan shape. Glue the sticks together at the bottom where they meet and let dry.

2. Lay the sticks on a piece of paper, and trace around the fan shape with a pencil. Cut out the fan shape and decorate it with cut-paper pieces.

3. Glue the paper fan on the ice-cream sticks. Make a ribbon bow, and glue it to the bottom of the fan.

LID CHICK MOBILE

(frozen-juice pull-top lids, poster board, construction paper, string, heavy paper plate)

1. For each small chick, trace around a frozen-juice pull-top lid twice on a piece of yellow poster board, and cut out the circles. Place the end of a long string on one side of each lid. Glue a circle to each side of the lids, keeping the string in the middle.

2. Fold a piece of orange paper in half. On the fold, cut out beaks and wings for each chick. With the folded ends pointing outward, glue the cut ends on each side of a chick. Add eyes with a marker.

3. Draw and cut out a large chick, and glue it to the back of a heavy paper plate. Add a beak and wings. Draw an eye.

4. Punch a hole at the top of the plate, and tie a loop of string for the hanger. Punch holes at the bottom of the plate and tie a chick to each hole.

WOVEN EGG BASKET
(construction paper)

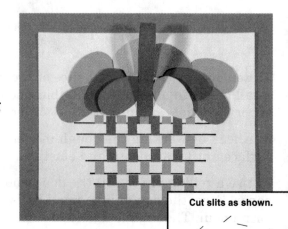

1. On a 9-by-12-inch sheet of construction paper, draw the lines as shown in the diagram to begin the basket. Cut along the lines with scissors.

2. Cut strips measuring 4 1/2 inches by 1/2 inch from two colors of paper. Weave these in and out of the slits to form a basket. Glue the ends in place.

3. Cut an 11-inch strip of paper for the handle. Bend in half and glue it to the basket.

4. Draw and cut out paper eggs, each with a tab as shown. Cut slits above the basket and slip the eggs in them. Turn over the sheet of paper, and glue the tabs of the eggs in place.

5. Bend the handle and eggs forward so they stand away from the background.

Cut slits as shown.

PETER COTTONTAIL

(plastic-foam cup, 2 1/2-inch plastic-foam ball, paper, broom straw, ribbon)

1. Glue a 2 1/2-inch plastic-foam ball to the bottom of a plastic-foam cup.

2. Cut paper eyes, a nose, and a mouth, and glue them to the ball to create the face. Make slits in the top of the head with a table knife and insert paper ears. Push in small pieces of broom straw for the whiskers.

3. Tie a ribbon bow around the neck. Add circles of ribbon for buttons. Glue a ring of ribbon to the bottom of the cup. Add a cotton-ball tail.

TUBE OF FLOWERS

(bathroom tissue tube, construction paper, cardboard, pipe cleaners)

1. Spread glue on a bathroom tissue tube, and cover it with paper. Cut a circle from a piece of cardboard for the base, and glue paper on top of it.

2. Glue the tube to the center of the base. Glue on a cut-paper flower.

3. Cut two flower shapes from paper for each flower. Place a pipe cleaner in between them and glue together.

4. Place the flowers in the tube.

TISSUE PAPER PLACE MATS

(white poster board, colored tissue paper, old newspaper, glue and water, plastic cup, paper towel, clear self-adhesive paper)

1. Cut a piece of white poster board to measure about 12 inches by 18 inches.

2. Cut colored tissue paper in the shapes of flower petals and leaves.

3. Cover your work surface with old newspaper. Mix white glue and some water in a plastic cup.

4. Place a tissue petal on a paper towel and brush it with the glue mixture. Place the petal on the poster board. Continue until your design is finished.

5. Cut a piece of clear self-adhesive paper larger than the poster board. Have someone help you remove the backing. Place the adhesive paper over your design. Fold the edges over to the back and trim if necessary.

EGG WITH CHICK MESSAGE
(construction paper)

1. Cut two eggs from orange construction paper. Print "Happy Easter" on one.

2. Place a small amount of glue around the side and bottom edges of the other egg. With "Happy Easter" on top, press the two eggs together, leaving an opening.

3. From yellow paper, cut out a chick to fit inside the opening. Write a message on the chick, and place it inside the egg with its head poking out.

RABBIT TABLE DECORATION
(construction paper)

1. Draw a rabbit in the center of a sheet of construction paper, making sure that it touches along the bottom.

2. Draw long strips on both sides of the bottom as shown.

3. Cut out the rabbit and the strips. Glue on paper ears, eyes, a nose, a mouth, whiskers, and front paws.

4. Pull the strips around to the back, overlap the ends, and staple or glue.

SPRING POUCH
(felt, paper towel, button)

Diagram 1

Flap

Fold
lines

Pouch

1. Cut a strip of felt 9 inches by 4 1/2 inches. Fold the felt strip as shown in Diagram 1, leaving a 2-inch flap at the top.

2. Glue along the sides to form a pouch. Place a paper towel on top and then a heavy book to hold the pouch in place until the glue dries.

Diagram 2

Slit

3. Sew a button to the pouch and cut a small slit in the flap as shown in Diagram 2. Button the pouch closed. Decorate with pieces of cut felt.

Button

LOLLIPOP FLOWER
(lollipop in cellophane, construction paper)

1. Use a medium-sized lollipop wrapped in cellophane for each flower.

2. Cut a strip of green construction paper 1/2 inch by 5 inches long for the stem. Glue one end of the strip at the bottom of the candy, and wind it around the stick. Glue it at the end. Add paper leaves. Hold the paper in place with paper clips if needed.

3. Cut out a 2-inch-round circle. Cut a small circle from the center. Trim around the edges to form a flower. Glue it on top of the candy. Round off the corners of the cellophane with scissors.

PLASTIC-FOAM CUP BUNNY
(two plastic-foam cups, poster board, paper, ribbon)

1. Turn one plastic-foam cup upside down and glue the side of another one to the top and let dry.

2. Cut two big ears and eyes from white poster board. Add pink paper to the ears and black paper to the eyes.

3. Cut a slit with a table knife along the rim of the cup and insert the ears. Cut a slit for each eye and push the paper eyes in place. Add glue to hold.

4. Cut a nose, mouth, and whiskers from paper. Attach them with glue. Tie a ribbon around the bunny's neck.

EASTER EGG BASKET
(facial tissue box, heavy white paper, poster paint, plastic grass)

1. Use a 3-by-9-by-5-inch facial tissue box for the base of the basket. Trim around the opening of the box so there is a 1-inch border.

2. Cut slits all the way around the border. Paint it to look like straw. Paint the rest of the box another color.

3. Cut two identical eggs from 8-by-10-inch pieces of heavy white paper. Cut a small opening at the top of the eggs for a handle. Decorate with markers. Glue the tops of the handles together.

4. Glue one egg to each side of the box. Hold in place with paper clips. Place plastic grass inside.

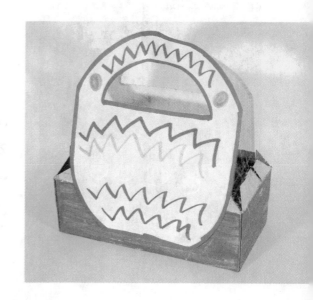

EASTER CHICK CARD
(construction paper)

1. Fold a piece of construction paper in the shape of a card. Write a message on the inside.

2. Cut a piece of paper to fit the width of the card, and make slits to look like grass. Glue it to the bottom of the card.

3. Draw and cut out a chick. Glue it standing in the grass.

COIN FLOWERS
(various coins, construction paper, markers)

1. Cut a vase shape from construction paper, and glue it to a large piece of construction paper.

2. Trace around the edges of quarters, dimes, nickels, and pennies to form flowers. Color the flowers with markers.

3. Draw stems and leaves to join the flowers to the vase.

BASKET BOX
(cereal box, construction paper, fabric, plastic grass)

1. Cut a cereal box as shown, removing the top flaps and a section of the front and the back of the box. Cover it with construction paper, taping it to hold in place.

2. Staple the side strips together to form a handle.

3. Cut small circles of fabric, and glue them on top of each other to form flowers. Glue them to the front of the box. Add a fabric bow and plastic grass.

HANDKERCHIEF BUNNY

(white handkerchief, buttons, thread, ribbon, juice glass)

1. Fold a large white handkerchief in half diagonally, as shown in the first diagram. Fold up the bottom of A and B about 2 inches.

2. Fold the points A and B over the middle of C as shown to form the bunny ears.

3. Turn the handkerchief over, and fold point C down to form the bunny head.

4. Gather the handkerchief together around the neck and tie a ribbon. Sew on two button eyes and thread for whiskers.

5. Place the bunny on a juice glass at Dad's place at the breakfast table for a surprise Easter gift.

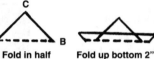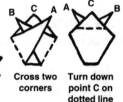

Fold in half   Fold up bottom 2"   Cross two corners   Turn down point C on dotted line

CHICK NEST

(6-inch paper plate, poster board, plastic grass, hard-boiled egg)

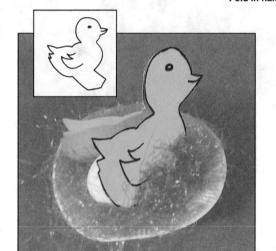

1. Cut two chicks as shown in the diagram from two 5-by-6-inch pieces of yellow poster board. Outline the edges and create eyes, a bill, and wings with black marker.

2. Glue the two heads together. Fold up the feet and glue them to the bottom of a 6-inch paper plate. Glue plastic grass around the chick.

3. Hard-boil an egg following the directions on page 32. Place the egg in between the two chicks and serve for breakfast.

RABBIT NUT CUP

(bathroom tissue tube, paper, paper baking cups)

1. Cut a 1 1/2-inch section from a bathroom tissue tube. Cover it with white paper.

2. Cut out a circle for the base, larger than the end of the tube. Glue the tube in the center of the circle and let dry.

3. Make a bow tie from a paper baking cup by creasing it in three evenly spaced places in the middle. Staple to hold it in place. Glue it on the edge of the circle.

4. Cut a paper baking cup in half and form the halves into two cone shapes for the ears. Glue them inside the tube. Add a rabbit face with markers and fill the cup with nuts.

BABY CHICK EASTER EGG
(construction paper, rickrack)

1. Fold a piece of construction paper in half for the card. Draw and cut out an egg from paper and glue it to the front of the card.

2. Draw and cut out a chick's head from paper, and glue it to the center of the egg.

3. Cut a small piece of rickrack, and glue it to the bottom of the chick as if the chick is peeping through a crack in the eggshell. Write a message inside.

FLUTED FLOWERPOT
(plastic margarine tub, 9-inch paper plate, ribbon, pipe cleaner, plant)

1. Glue the bottom of a round plastic margarine tub to the center of a 9-inch paper plate and let dry. Cut flaps every 2 or 3 inches from the outer edge of the plate to the bottom of the tub.

2. Bend up the flaps, and glue them to the tub. Hold the paper plate in place with a rubber band until it has dried, and glue a ribbon in its place. Add small bows to the sides.

3. For a handle, insert two pipe cleaners, twisted together, into holes on opposite sides of the tub. Twist the ends tightly.

4. Fill the container with a small potted plant.

BRANCH WREATH
(branches, leftover non-paste wallpaper, rubber band)

1. Take several thin branches, and bend the ends together to form an egg-shaped wreath. You may need someone to help hold the ends together as you place a heavy rubber band around them.

2. Cut strips of non-paste wallpaper, and glue the ends together to make a long ribbon. Wrap the ribbon around the wreath and glue the ends.

3. Cut out wallpaper eggs and glue them to the wreath.

4. To make the bow, cut strips of wallpaper about 12 inches in length. Glue the ends of each strip together to form a circle. Staple the round strip in the middle, forming a figure 8. Do this with several strips.

5. Place the stapled strips on top of each other to form a bow, and staple all of them together in the middle. Glue or tie the bow to the wreath.

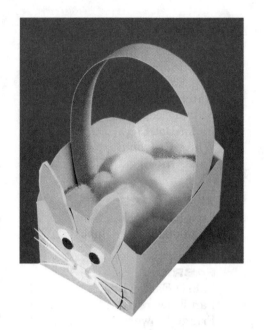

PAPER-RABBIT BASKET
(construction paper, cotton balls)

1. Draw the pattern shown on a 9-by-12-inch piece of construction paper. Cut along the solid lines.

2. Set aside the narrow strip at the edge to be used for the handle.

3. Fold up the sides and ends of the basket on the dotted lines. Glue together the ends marked A, then the ends marked B. This will make a little box.

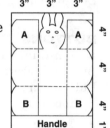

4. Fold up the head and tail, and glue in place. Add a face with cut paper and a cotton-ball tail. Fill the basket with more cotton balls.

EGG RABBIT
(hard-boiled egg, cotton ball, heavy white paper)

1. Make a hard-boiled egg, following the directions given on page 32.

2. From heavy white paper, cut two ears, two small front legs, and two large back legs and glue them on the egg. Add a cotton-ball tail.

3. Draw a face with markers.

RABBIT CARD HOLDER
(two 9-inch paper plates, yarn, construction paper)

1. Cut away a small section of two 9-inch paper plates. These will be the rabbit's ears.

2. Place the larger sections of the plates together face to face. Staple around the edges, leaving the cut edges open.

3. For the face, cut out construction paper eyes, a nose, and a mouth and glue to one side of the plate. Add yarn whiskers. With a stapler, attach the ears to the plate in back of the face.

4. Tape a yarn loop to the back. Hang the holder, and place your Easter cards inside.

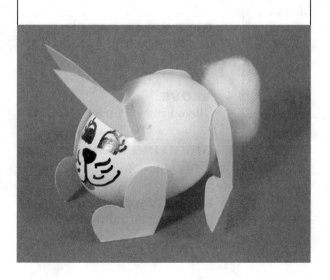

MATERIAL INDEX